LIVING FRUITFULLY CHASTITY

Learning from the Saints

by
Fr John McKeever

*All booklets are published thanks to the
generous support of the members of the
Catholic Truth Society*

CATHOLIC TRUTH SOCIETY
PUBLISHERS TO THE HOLY SEE

*"I betrothed you to Christ, thinking to present you as
a chaste virgin to her true and only husband"*
(*2 Co* 11:2)

All rights reserved. First published 2017 by The Incorporated Catholic
Truth Society 40-46 Harleyford Road London SE11 5AY Tel: 020
7640 0042 Fax: 020 7640 0040 © 2017 The Incorporated Catholic
Truth Society.

ISBN 978 1 78469 200 1

Contents

Introduction

Chastity is a term that is rarely heard nowadays. It may seem dated or even irrelevant in an era when sexual attitudes and behaviour are liberal and very much regarded as one's own business. The idea of having a set of rules or even a virtue to regulate sexual behaviour is unthinkable to many. Moreover, chastity is sometimes confused with celibacy, which is the choice not to marry and therefore to abstain permanently from sexual relations. Chastity does not mean simply not having sex. It means living sexuality in accordance with the truth of our human nature as it was created by God. This includes avoiding sex with anyone who is not one's spouse. But it also means knowing how best to love one's spouse, regulate one's fertility in a moral manner, and to live one's sexual identity as a man or woman in a way that respects one's own dignity and the dignity of everybody else. It is a way of loving that gives joy and life. As Pope St John Paul II said, "Only the chaste man and the chaste woman are capable of true love".

So what is the Catholic Church's understanding of chastity? The great intellectual genius and teacher of the faith, St Thomas Aquinas (1225-1274) simply called it the moderation of sexuality in accordance with reason, that is, with its natural purpose and meaning. The Youth Catechism of the Catholic Church defines it as "the virtue by which a person who is capable of passion deliberately and resolutely reserves his erotic desires for love and resists the temptation to find lewd images in the media or to use others as a means of achieving his own satisfaction".[1] These temptations are very prevalent today because, even if as the song says "Love is all around me", sex is too! It is used in advertising, in pop music, in fashion and magazines because, according to the old slogan, "Sex sells". Contraception is readily available, thus promoting the message that casual sex is normal. Television shows (especially reality TV) and movies have become more explicit and the internet is flooded with pornography and other sexual material. The result is that children are becoming sexualised at an ever younger age. Even ordinary men and women who in past decades could have avoided the explicit material only available in "adult" shops, can now consume what previously they wouldn't have been seen dead looking for, simply by clicking on an icon on their computer or smartphone.

How to Use this Book

This booklet is offered as a help to counter this sexualisation and the misery it often brings through addiction, abuse, exploitation, broken hearts and even sexually transmitted infections. Chastity is not only holy, it is healthy. The Church is ever concerned with what is good for humanity, what makes for genuine flourishing and happiness. As a mother, the Church wants all her children to be able to love and have peace, joy and stability in their lives. In the words of Psalm 128, she wants people to be able to live as husband and wife in the heart of their house, with children as shoots of the olive around their table, living to see their children's children in a secure city.

Chastity is not just a virtue that is achieved by practice and moral effort. It is also a fruit of the Holy Spirit, to be acquired as part of a prayerful, spiritual life, depending on the help of God and not on our own strength. This booklet will try to explain chastity in the light of the working of the Holy Spirit in one's life. It will also offer some suggestions for living chastity well and some help for those who may be struggling in the area of sexual morality so that they can find freedom and peace. In particular, it will draw upon the wisdom and experience of those who managed to master not only chastity but the art of holiness, sometimes at a great cost: the saints. Sexuality and chastity are part of every person's life story. Let us begin with one of the most remarkable life stories of all: the conversion of St Augustine.

A Moral Miracle

"Lord, give me chastity and continence, but not yet!" This infamous prayer of the young Augustine of Hippo (354-430) reflects the inner conflict of any soul who recognises the virtuous thing to do, yet fears the demanding struggle against human urges and passions. In his *Confessions*, St Augustine was not afraid to admit his utter powerlessness in the face of sexual temptation. As a young man, he had given in to the attraction of sexual pleasure and took a lover whom he would never marry but who bore him his only son, Adeodatus. He was brutally honest about why he chose to live with this woman: "I had chosen her for no special reason but that my restless passions had alighted on her". He was faithful to her throughout their years together, yet he could see that his love for her, marked by lust, was very different from the love he would expect in a proper marriage. This difference was most apparent in the attitude to children. Whereas marriage is contracted for the purpose of being open to new life, his irregular union was "a bargain struck for lust, in which the birth of children is begrudged, though, if they come, we cannot help but love them".

When Augustine abandoned the Catholic faith of his youth, much to the anxiety and dismay of his mother, St Monica, he never ceased to search for truth, even if his search led him down a few blind alleys. This search was hampered not just by his lack of understanding but by the power of the favourite sin which blinded him. His conversion was delayed because his sin enslaved him and prevented him from surrendering to the truth of the Catholic faith which would, in turn, have meant the abandonment of his old sinful lifestyle. He wrote: "I was bound down by this disease of the flesh. Its deadly pleasures were a chain that I dragged along with me, yet I was afraid to be freed from it". His friend, the chaste Alypius, tried to talk good sense into Augustine. However, vice is contagious, and curiosity together with Augustine's ideas began to lead Alypius astray: "For my part, I was a prisoner of habit, suffering cruel torments through trying to satisfy a lust that could never be sated: while Alypius was being led by curiosity into a like state of captivity".

The Power of a Mother's Tears

The power of sin enchained Augustine and used him as a net to ensnare others, but a far greater power was already at work. His saintly mother, Monica, had been praying for him for years with such weeping and longing that her local bishop reassured her: "Go in peace. It cannot be that the son of these tears should be lost." Monica followed him to Milan, intensifying the outpouring of her tears and prayers. She could see that the good influence of St Ambrose's teaching was weakening her son's resistance but that he still had a great crisis to pass through before he would be converted. She tried to organise a marriage for Augustine to a suitably Catholic lady and so managed to get him to leave his lover. This attempt at virtue only revealed how weak and vice-ridden Augustine really was. He later recalled:

> Meanwhile I was sinning more and more. The woman with whom I had been living was torn from my side as an obstacle to my marriage and this was a blow which crushed my heart to bleeding, because I loved her dearly. She went back to Africa, vowing never to give herself to any other man … But I was too unhappy and too weak to imitate this example set me by a woman. I was impatient at the delay of two years that had to pass before the girl I had asked to marry became my wife, and because I was more a slave of lust than a true lover of marriage, I took another mistress, without the sanction of wedlock. This meant that the disease of

my soul would continue unabated, in fact it would persist into the state of marriage.

His fiancée had a lucky escape, being spared marriage to this immature, sex-obsessed cheat. Monica's prayers, the influence of Ambrose and his spiritual father Simplicianus, and the designs of God's providence intervened to convert the sinner into a saint. Augustine was already being swayed to embrace the truth of the Catholic faith, yet his mind was being held back by the sinful habits that bound his will. He knew the truth, but he could not pay the price for this great treasure, that is, the renunciation of his sins, especially sexual immorality. He admitted:

I was quite sure that it was better for me to give myself up to your love than to surrender to my own lust. But while I wanted to follow the first course and was convinced that it was right, I was still a slave to the pleasures of the second.

The Brink of Resolution

Liberation came as suddenly as it was unexpected. One day, a senior official from the imperial court came to visit Augustine and chatted to him about the wonderful life of St Antony of Egypt, saying it had convinced him that it was far better to be a friend of God than of the Emperor. These words struck a chord with Augustine. Suddenly, he could see himself as he really was: sordid and miserable. He could no longer turn a blind eye to the sin he knew all too well. His conscience gnawed at him and he was overcome with shame. At this point, Augustine grew unsettled, frantic, like a man on the verge of a nervous breakdown. Grace and nature were at war within him and he could take no more! He knew that only a small chain held him back from converting. By his own willpower he tried to break it, repeating "Let it be now, let it be now!" St Augustine's words may well strike a chord with all those who struggle to make that last, definitive, break with their past:

> I was on the point of making it but I did not succeed. … I stood on the brink of resolution, waiting to take fresh breath. I tried again and came a little nearer to my goal, and then a little nearer still, so that I could almost reach out and grasp it. But I did not reach it … My lower instincts, which had taken firm hold of me, were stronger than the higher.

In his mind, Augustine saw the beauty of Chastity approaching, beckoning him. She seemed to say: "Why do you try to stand in your own strength and fail? Cast yourself upon God and have no fear. He will not shrink away and let you fall … he will welcome you and cure you of your ills." He retreated to the garden in tears, seeking to hide from his friends, when he heard a child's voice say, "Take it and read". So he took up the Bible beside him and opened it at random. His eyes immediately fell upon these words of St Paul: "Let us behave decently, as in the daytime, not in carousing and drunkenness, not in sexual immorality and debauchery, not in dissension and jealousy. Rather, clothe yourselves with the Lord Jesus Christ, and do not think about how to gratify the desires of the flesh" (*Rm* 13:13-14). In an instant, his heart was flooded with light and he was filled with faith and love for God. He no longer desired a wife or any earthly pleasure.

Transformed and Uplifted by Grace

Augustine received baptism from St Ambrose and eventually became a priest and bishop. Although he never relapsed into his former ways, the struggle for chastity never fully left him. In *Confessions*, he admitted to the impure thoughts and temptations that still assailed him in later life: "The load of habit is a force to be reckoned with". When a man converts, he is never fully changed. Some of his old nature stays with him. This is the price that grace demands, for grace builds upon nature, and if some aspects of our nature still incline us to sin, these same aspects, transformed and uplifted by grace, can also become instruments of God's good work. While Augustine's nature was still strong enough to make him struggle for purity, even requiring him to ban all visits of women from his monastery and never be alone with them, that same nature was used by God to sing of his praises and preach his word with all the untamed passion of a lover! His passion never changed, only its direction. The same is true of many of the saints. St Francis of Assisi (1181/2-1226) experienced the usual hot bloodedness of youth. In a sense, he never lost it, as he used to warn those who heaped adulation upon him: "Do not canonise me too quickly, I am perfectly capable of fathering a child". Like St Augustine, Francis would have a strict Rule to preserve his chastity and that of his brothers. He would always take care not to look a woman in the face or be left alone with her, St Clare included. "The company of women is poisoned honey", he warned, because he knew the old desires still burned strongly within him. As the novelist Julien Green aptly observed: "We remain what we are till death – turn a glove inside out and it's still a glove. The saint and sinner are reunited in the same coffin."

The power that enabled St Augustine, St Francis and so many other saints to undergo such a radical conversion from sexual impurity to chastity is the only power that can help any of us overcome the temptations that are part and parcel of our human nature: the power of God's grace. St Paul told the Galatians that we are set free from sin by Christ through the power of his Holy Spirit dwelling within us. Without the Holy Spirit, we are as helpless in the battle for chastity as Augustine was. In this booklet we will look at chastity as a fruit of the Holy Spirit, paying particular attention to how this fruit is inseparable from all the others. By striving to use the weapons of the Spirit which the saints used to reach the chastity which is meant for all Christians, our whole life of faith can become clearer and easier. For the brightness of purity comes from the light of Truth, which has been revealed to us in Christ and poured into our hearts through the Holy Spirit, who has been given to us (Cf. *Rm* 5:5).

Life in the Spirit

When we speak about the "fruits of the Holy Spirit", we are examining the "end product" of the spiritual life. A fruit is always both the end product and the new beginning in the cycle of life. Take, for example, any normal fruit. If one wishes to harvest fruits, one must first go through the long process of planting a seed or sapling, nurturing it, fertilising, feeding and watering it, perhaps sheltering it at some stages, until the plant, vine or tree is mature and able to produce fruit. Depending on the type of plant or tree in question, this process might take months or years. The end goal is the harvesting of the fruit, to be eaten and enjoyed. But this fruit also contains seeds that can be collected and used to plant further fruit trees so that one's harvest will continue to grow as time progresses. We can look at the fruits of the Holy Spirit in the same way. The Catechism calls them "perfections that the Holy Spirit forms in us as the first fruits of eternal glory".[2] Following St Jerome's translation of the Bible, the Catechism enumerates twelve fruits: charity, joy, peace, patience, kindness, goodness, generosity, gentleness, faithfulness, modesty, self-control and chastity (CCC 1832). They are, in this world, the first manifestations (or first fruits) of that beautiful life which we will experience perfectly in heaven, that is, our new life in the Risen Christ.

When St Paul listed the fruits of the Holy Spirit, he was describing the end result of the process he described in Romans 6, dying to the old ways of sin in baptism where we join Christ in his death, so that we can also rise with him to new life. Those who are reborn in baptism and share Christ's life should live the same kind of life as Christ lived (*1 Jn* 2:6), for if we don't live in union with him here and now, how can we hope to share in his life for eternity? This is why Paul contrasted the worldly way of life he called "the works of the flesh" (*Ga* 5:19) with the godly way of life he called "the fruit of the Spirit". He stressed that we shall reap what we sow. If we sow to please the flesh, we shall reap a harvest of corruption, but if we sow in the Spirit, we will reap a harvest of eternal life from the Spirit (*Ga* 6:7-8).

Chastity is a Form of Love

Paul actually used the term "fruit" in the singular (*karpos*) to signify that this is one unified way of life springing from the root of faith in Christ. In this sense, the twelve "fruits" are really more like twelve segments of the one orange, or twelve petals of the one flower. They may have a certain variety, but an even more profound unity. One fruit cannot exist without the others. Just as Plato and Aquinas said that one could not truly have one of the cardinal virtues (prudence, justice, fortitude, temperance) without the others because each supports the others and dovetails into them, so too does Paul imply that one could not simply bear a couple of these qualities and ignore the others. St Paul wrote elsewhere, "To me, life is Christ" (*Ph* 1:21). The fruit of the Holy Spirit is simply this unified, holy life which is Christ. It is the portrait of Jesus, replicated in the lives of those who are united to him in faith, by the power of the Holy Spirit. As the Catechism teaches, "The mission of the Spirit of adoption is to unite believers to Christ and make them live in him".[3]

Even at a casual glance we can see that chastity includes the other fruits and depends upon them, so that it appears to be the crown of the fruits of the Holy Spirit. Chastity is a form of love. It brings joy and peace. It requires patience, as chaste love waits for a committed relationship before making that mutual self-gift of the body. By freeing one from inordinate and blinding passion, it allows the flourishing of love that is focused on the needs of the other and so it makes room for kindness, goodness, gentleness and generosity. Chaste love is faithful and it requires modesty and self-control for its very existence.

Jesus himself fully explained the mission of the Holy Spirit in his final discourse at the Last Supper. He stressed that the Spirit's work was intimately tied to his own: "He will glorify me, for everything that he makes known to you he will draw from what is mine" (*Jn* 16:14). The life the Spirit teaches and manifests in us is a glorification of Christ, making his image shine forth within us. That is why the papal preacher, Fr Raniero Cantalamessa OFM, called the fruits of the Holy Spirit "Christological fruits", signs of a close relationship with Christ. Jesus said that those who abide in him would bear much fruit (*Jn* 15:5) and that they would perform the same kind of works he did himself. Indeed, he said they would perform even greater works because he was going to the Father (*Jn* 14:12) and unless he goes to the Father the Holy Spirit will not come (*Jn* 16:7), thus showing our need of the Holy Spirit in order to be able to live Christ-like lives. Jesus also called the Holy Spirit "Advocate" (literally "Helper" in the widest sense of the Greek word *parakléton*), showing the Spirit will help Christians to know *and* do what Christ commands and live their baptismal identity as "other Christs".

The Fruit of Good Actions

How does the Holy Spirit produce his fruits in a Christian's life? St Thomas Aquinas understood the fruits to be a form of direct action in us on the part of the Spirit. He described human beings as the trees which produce the fruit of good actions. If one's actions are the result of human reasoning, they can be said to be the "fruit" of one's reason. But if they come from a higher power, that is, from the Holy Spirit, then they can be said to be the fruit of the Holy Spirit. Virtues are good habits which we have built up as the result of many good choices, having made right use of human reason; whereas the fruits of the Holy Spirit are acts which the Spirit inspires directly in us. We have already seen an example of this in the conversion of St Augustine. By his use of human reason, he tried to break free from his old habits and embrace the Catholic way of life he knew to be true, but he was not strong enough on his own to develop the virtue of chastity and so be truly free. He needed that sudden impulse of grace to pull him free and make him embrace chastity. This was an action of the Holy Spirit. However, we can never separate chastity as a fruit of the Holy Spirit from chastity as a virtue. The fruit may be compared to a booster rocket, propelling a person beyond the force of the sinful habit (which we call *vice*) that binds them. Unless the person proceeds to develop good habits of virtue, however, the force of the old habits, like gravity, will pull them back down. We must cooperate with God's grace. Time and again, if one slips and falls back, God's grace is there in Confession to grant pardon and strength for a new beginning. The Holy Spirit may inject the repentant sinner with his fruit once again to get them back on the wagon. But without a commitment to pursue the virtue of chastity, there can be no final victory.

Cantalamessa has described the fruits of the Holy Spirit as the end result when our human freedom cooperates with divine grace: "The fruits are produced when the garden of our liberty receives the dew of the Holy Spirit". As with all fruits, the seeds must be harvested and sown again so that the cycle of life can continue and a new harvest be reaped. The seeds of our initial victories in chastity, won by the Holy Spirit's action in us, need to be carefully tended and cultivated by means of perseverance in the spiritual life and the building up of good habits. At the same time, we must be careful to avoid the pitfalls of past mistakes and shun the occasions of sin (i.e., any circumstances or company that could lead us into temptations we'd find hard to resist) that could revive our vicious habits and snuff out the little fire of virtue the Spirit has kindled in the soul. So the fruits of the Spirit cannot be separated from the moral virtues. They exist to serve and nurture them. We must never think we have ever grown so strong in virtue as to no longer need the input of the fruits of the Holy Spirit. That would be a very dangerous manifestation of pride. While human beings can acquire certain virtuous habits by means of their own effort, they can never reach the holiness Christ called us to when he said "Be perfect as your heavenly Father is perfect" (*Mt* 5:48). Indeed, he warned, "Apart from me you can do nothing" (*Jn* 15:5). At the end of the day, our final goal is to be a saint, and saints are never self-made. They are God's work of art, the masterpiece of the Holy Spirit who the Church calls *digitus Paternae dexterae*: the finger of God's right hand.

Moulded into the Image of Christ

St John Paul II, St Josemaría Escrivá, St Francis de Sales and so many of the saints have taught consistently that holiness is meant for everyone, not an elite few. Therefore, the fruits of the Holy Spirit, including chastity, are meant for everyone, whatever their age, vocation or state in life. In this respect, the fruits of the Holy Spirit must be distinguished from the charisms that the Holy Spirit gives, such as the gifts of teaching or preaching, prophecy, administration, etc.[4] There are many different gifts to support the variety of roles in the Church and no one can possibly do them all. Each Christian has his or her special role to play in the building up of the Body of Christ, the Church. Everyone does, however, receive the seven gifts of the Holy Spirit in addition to the twelve fruits. These gifts are wisdom, understanding, counsel, fortitude, knowledge, piety and fear of the Lord. Whereas the fruits are specific actions, the gifts are permanent dispositions which make a believer open and obedient in following the promptings of the Holy Spirit. We could say they prepare us for and dispose us to receive the fruits. They also help us to cooperate with the fruits and so turn them into a permanent feature of our character: into virtues. As the Catechism teaches, the seven gifts "belong in their fullness to Christ, the Son of David. They complete and perfect the virtues of those who receive them. They make the faithful docile in readily obeying divine inspirations."[5]

This process of being moulded into the image of Christ will inevitably lead us to an encounter with the cross. In later chapters, we will look at the challenges we must face and the spiritual tools and remedies that can be used for growth in chastity. But first we must look at chastity in itself and see how this sadly neglected and even despised quality can truly be said to be a gift from God, a fruit of the Holy Spirit.

The Beauty of Chastity

It is a great pity that our sex-obsessed culture with its pursuit of pleasure as the be all and end all of a fulfilling life has banished chastity as something outdated or even laughable, suitable only for old maids, prudes and simpletons. So many people in their pursuit of sex are just like St Augustine: they are searching for love and for happiness. They are enthralled by physical beauty and charm but the greatest beauty of all is inside us, in our character. Love, beauty and happiness cannot be truly found apart from chastity.

True love is chaste: it respects oneself and one's beloved and so places limits on desire so that the other is truly loved for their own good and not just as a means of satisfying one's own needs or desires. Chastity is also beautiful because it reflects the perfect love of heaven where everything is beautiful and where there is no marrying or begetting children but where human beings live and love like the angels (*Mt* 22: 29-30). And chastity is happiness because "love" that's really barely disguised lust or self-indulgence causes, deep down, a disgust with one's selfishness or enslavement to animal appetites. Without the self-respect that comes from virtuous living, one cannot be truly happy. Even after the sweetest illicit sexual pleasure, there is always awaiting any soul that has not completely killed his conscience a certain emptiness, disappointment and sense of guilt: the bitter dregs of the sweetest cup!

This emptiness is not a uniquely Catholic, or even religious, phenomenon. It is a natural human sensation and as such it has been well documented in great literature. One striking example is Hermann Hesse's novel, *Narcissus and Goldmund,* where the young student Goldmund wanders the country searching for fulfilment in all forms of beauty and ecstasy, including innumerable illicit love affairs. Hesse describes Goldmund's passion and rapturous anticipation before his sexual encounters and the sadness that inevitably follows each one, for example: "In both of them a great sadness welled up, from which they fled into sleep". Eventually, Goldmund realises his sadness comes from the fact that sexual pleasures do not last. He is aiming for something great, even eternal, but finds only a pleasure that fails to satisfy because it is fleeting yet mercilessly compels him to seek it again and again.

The love of women, sexual games – these had priority for him, and the core of his frequent bouts of melancholy and jaded spirits grew from his knowledge of the fleeting nature of lust. The swift, delicious surge of ecstasy, its brief, rapturous blaze, its rapid extinction – this seemed to him to comprise the core of all experience; this became for him the image of all bliss and all suffering.

No wonder Shakespeare could personify all lust in Cleopatra with these few words: "She makes hungry where most she satisfies".

Banish the Dark Clouds

Real life abounds with evidence to corroborate literature's insights into the bond between chastity and happiness. Dawn Eden, the renowned author on chastity, was raised a secular Jew, without any guilt about masturbation yet she still felt uncomfortable and associated it with a kind of despair:

It was, at best, a wilful self-medication against the pain of loneliness, and it always came with a cost. The cost was having to repress the ever-deepening awareness that all the physical pleasure in the world could not compensate for the absence of someone who would love me for who I was.

A simple internet search for the terms "masturbation" and "feeling guilty" will show she is far from alone. St Josemaría Escrivá (1902-1975), the founder of Opus Dei, was a spiritual director to many souls. From them, he knew the sufferings that unchastity can bring. He wrote, "When you have sought the company of a sensual satisfaction, what loneliness afterward!"

The truth about love and chastity is embedded in our human nature. One can try to dull the voice of the natural law in one's conscience by trying to rationalise the guilt away, saying, "It's not really a big sin" or "Sure, everybody's doing it". Or one can try to chase away that nagging sense of unease and unhappiness by drinking or using drugs, by seeking comfort in worldly things such as possessions, parties and exotic holidays, or by spending a fortune on "non-directive" counselling or psychotherapy where one wants to be reassured "You're ok as you are". One can even try to quell the misery by seeking more and more sex, a more powerful orgasm, a better partner. All to no avail! As a wise priest once said, "I have never met a truly happy person who was unchaste or a chaste person who was generally profoundly unhappy".

Fruits are something to be savoured and enjoyed. So too with chastity as a fruit of the Holy Spirit: it is a fruit that is beautiful and pleasing to the mind. It has a sweet savour and brings its own enjoyment. It is fulfilling and healthy, both physically and spiritually. It helps banish the dark clouds of melancholy and depression.

The Total Gift of Yourself

Chastity means respecting the fact that sexuality has three aspects that must belong together: fruitfulness, which means openness to having children; mutual love, which of its essence must be true, faithful and permanent; and sexual pleasure which is something good and beautiful, not to be despised by negative or prudish attitudes to the body. When all three are integrated in one's sexuality so that none are excluded, one can claim to be living chastely.

Those who are married may exercise their mutual right and duty to sexual intercourse when they respect this unity within sex as it was created by God. Those who are not married cannot claim that their love is faithful and permanent as they have not bound themselves in the indissoluble bonds of marriage: they are still free to leave. Whereas sexual intercourse is a physical expression of the total self-giving of the person in love, to engage in that act outside of marriage would be an untruth as one has not really given oneself fully and permanently by means of marriage vows. In the words of St John Paul II, "To give your body to another person symbolises the total gift of yourself to that person".[6] Moreover, because they have not formed a secure and permanent family life by means of marriage, unmarried couples are not in the best position to bring children into the world either. Hence they must abstain from intercourse, which is naturally meant for procreation, and from all impure actions that could so easily lead to sex.

All that is left, then, is sexual pleasure. Sexuality based on the pleasure principle alone would be reduced to a form of mutual self-indulgence, perhaps with sincere *feelings* of affection-love, but still without the self-sacrifice of gift-love inherent in the promise of committing definitively to one person for life, forsaking all others. Indeed, should sexual pleasure be permitted as a good in itself, simply for its own sake alone, there is no reason why it should be restricted to marriage or indeed to any form of relationship. It would be reduced from a means of expressing true, selfless love to pure self-indulgence. This is what the Catechism calls the sin of *lust*: "Lust is disordered desire for or inordinate enjoyment of sexual pleasure. Sexual pleasure is morally disordered when sought for itself, isolated from its procreative and unitive purposes."[7] Unchastity, or lust, can take many forms. It is the sin of *fornication* if the man and woman are single, *adultery* if at least one of them is married or *sacrilege* if one of them is consecrated to God in the priesthood or religious life. Moreover, any other form of genital sexual expression outside of marriage is also sinful for the same reasons that they cannot fulfil that integration of the threefold aspects of sexuality. The Catechism lists these other offences against chastity: masturbation,[8] pornography,[9] prostitution,[10] rape[11] and homosexual actions.[12]

The Gift of Chastity

Chastity is not merely the avoidance of these sins. It is a virtue to be desired and cultivated simply for its own sake, because it is good and makes us love more genuinely, becoming more like Christ. Chastity, as a fruit of the Holy Spirit, is an inspired taste or attraction. It means seeing the beauty of true love and, being enraptured by the beauty of truth, pursuing it wholeheartedly. Chastity cannot live without beauty, otherwise it would not be desirable. Indeed, how could anything the Spirit creates in us not be loveable and desirable? We still have a tendency to think of chastity in negative terms as a compendium of sexual prohibitions. A long list of "Thou shalt nots", however true it may be, is not particularly motivating or inspiring. And if we focus only on our failures or on the height of the challenges and temptations that our weakness must face, we will be tempted to despair and surrender. We need a great *"Sursum corda!"*: "Lift up your hearts!" And to lift them up to the Lord: to Christ who is himself perfect Love, the most worthy object of our desire and the model of perfect chastity. Similarly we need to look to Our Lady, the Virgin most chaste and Mother most loveable, and to the saints who knew well the struggle to resist sexual temptation and remain chaste but who won the battle thanks to God's grace. They can teach and encourage us do the same. In the chapter on "Weapons and Remedies" we will look more closely at the example of the saints. For now, I would like to focus on the teaching of two great saints in order to better understand what chastity is and why it is so necessary: St Benedict (480-547), the father of western monasticism, and the great Dominican scholar who had a heart as pure as his mind was strong, St Thomas Aquinas.

St Benedict lived in the licentious atmosphere of Rome before giving up his career in the civil service for the spiritual and austere life of a monk at Subiaco. He later gained followers and founded the great abbey of Monte Cassino, giving birth to the Benedictine monastic family. He wrote a Rule for his monks, passing on to them the wisdom he had discovered. Benedict used only two words in his Rule concerning chastity: *Castitatem amare,* "to love chastity". This encourages us to look upon chastity in an entirely positive light. As a contemporary Benedictine scholar and blogger, Dom Mark Daniel Kirby OSB, has written: "Saint Benedict approaches chastity in an entirely positive way: it is something to be loved. A man loves what makes him happy. A man loves what contents his heart's desire. A man loves what he has experienced as being good for him." This in itself is important. The Desert Fathers knew that the battle against any sin or for any virtue is won or lost in the heart and mind, long before thoughts and desires have borne fruit in action. A positive mindset regarding chastity is essential, avoiding both the negative derision of our promiscuous culture and a fear or hatred of the body that could lead to sexual repression. We should look to God, the Creator of the body and of human love, who made these things to be good. Chastity must have been one of the things St Paul had in mind when he wrote: "Whatever is true, whatever is noble, whatever is right, whatever is pure, whatever is lovely, whatever is admirable – if anything is excellent or praiseworthy – think about such things" (*Ph* 4:8).

Chastity as a Virtue

Chastity, as a virtue, means bringing the order of reason to bear on the area of sexuality. The best passion to help us tame the passions of the body is the desire for truth, and this requires not just a pure heart but a well formed mind. When St Benedict tells us to "love chastity" he is directing us to think clearly about our human nature, about the purpose and goal of human sexuality as God has created it and to do so with regard to all its dimensions: physical (how sexual biology is designed to work), emotional (how sex is related to love and feelings) and spiritual (how sex serves to communicate the love of God and makes people sharers in the continuance of God's creation). This is also what Aquinas taught when he saw chastity as the virtue that brings sexuality under the power of reason. To keep sex in line with reason simply means to see it in a way that corresponds to reality. "Reality" includes the truth about the threefold purpose of sex, the truth about the moral nature and dignity of the human person as revealed by Scripture and by our own thinking about the natural law, and the demands of justice.

Indeed, the importance of justice in the area of chastity cannot be overlooked. As sexuality is lived in relationship, we cannot overlook what is "owed" to others as their due. For example, fidelity is owed to one's spouse and children as a matter of justice. Celibacy for a priest is owed to God and the Church as he has made a public promise to them. Chaste conduct prior to marriage is owed not only to one's partner (to "use" another for personal pleasure is itself unjust, even if both partners mutually agree to use each other) but also to society in general. As society has a legitimate interest in ensuring a secure future for itself through stable families with well looked after and morally educated children, it too has the right to claim in justice that the life-giving power of sexuality be properly respected by chaste behaviour.

If truth helps us to love chastity, the opposite is also true. Unchastity destroys our appreciation of the truth: it makes us blind to spiritual realities (as some reject God because they cannot live by his laws). Even our ability to see matters as they really are and make prudent decisions based upon right understanding of the facts can be hindered. As the great Catholic philosopher Josef Pieper explained, "unchastity begets a blindness of spirit which practically excludes all understanding of the goods of the spirit; unchastity splits the power of decision; conversely, the virtue of chastity more than any other makes man capable and ready for contemplation". Although the "purity of heart" mentioned in the Beatitudes is much broader than chastity because it means being totally focused upon God, it is still true that one cannot achieve this unity of focus if one's heart is divided by unchastity. If one wishes to advance in prayer, contemplation and understanding of heavenly things, one must ask for the grace of chastity and strive to cooperate with it. Even when we are dealing with earthly and not spiritual realities, we need chastity in order to have a clear head.

"Sin Makes You Stupid"

A priest friend of mine says "Sin makes you stupid" and in a sense he's right. One may have a powerful theoretical intellect, but if one's mind is clouded by sinful passions one will be a fool. The selfishness of the will cannot but intrude on the workings of the mind so that one will see reality as one wants to see it, not as it actually is. This in turn has consequences on the choices one makes, for example, when intelligent people make awful errors of judgement in choosing a lover or spouse which others can see clearly. Passions or any psychological wound which causes the need for affection or sex can blind reason. Again, Pieper explains this perfectly:

> Unchaste abandon and the self-surrender of the soul to the world of sensuality paralyzes the primordial powers of the moral person: the ability to perceive, in silence, the call of reality and to make, in the retreat of this silence, the decision appropriate to the concrete situation of concrete action. [...] An unchaste man wants, above all, something for himself; he is distracted by an unobjective "interest"; his constantly strained will-to-pleasure prevents him from confronting reality with that selfless detachment which alone makes genuine knowledge possible.

Aquinas compared an unchaste man to a lion who, seeing a stag, can see nothing but its dinner! Rushing blindly where passion leads rather than being able to stand back and objectively question whether this course of action is wise and good, he can't take time to weigh up the pros and cons. Such is the path to many a regretted one night stand or even the ruination from taking a dating relationship too far too soon.

Unchastity does not merely make a person unwise. One of modern England's greatest thinkers, the Oxbridge philosopher Elizabeth Anscombe, wrote in her famous pamphlet *Contraception and Chastity*:

> There is no such thing as a casual, non-significant sexual act; everyone knows this. ... Those who try to make room for sex as mere casual enjoyment pay the penalty: they become shallow. At any rate the talk that reflects and commends this attitude is always shallow. They dishonour their own bodies; holding cheap what is naturally connected with the origination of human life.

Moreover, with shallowness comes misery: a progressive lack of depth and satisfaction with sex and even life itself.

Reflection on Chastity

To conclude, the beauty of chastity and the dangers of unchastity have been summed up very well by Dom Mark Kirby in the following reflection. It bears much pondering and careful rereading:

Chastity leads to hope and to joy;
unchastity leads to despair and sadness.
Chastity delights God,
unchastity delights the devil.
Chastity opens the soul to God;
unchastity opens the soul to the devil.
Therefore, as Saint Benedict says,
    Castitatem amare,
"Love Chastity."

Chastity facilitates growth in all the other virtues;
unchastity stunts growth in all the virtues
and, if unchecked, will contaminate and
   destroy them.
Chastity opens the door to Divine intimacy;
unchastity closes the door to Divine intimacy,
attracts evil spirits,
and provides ground for familiarity with them.

Chastity confers spiritual authority
and causes the soul to radiate
   a supernatural peace.
Unchastity destroys spiritual authority
and causes the soul to emit a sense of disquiet,
   trouble and sadness.

Chastity is its own reward
in that it disposes the soul for familiar and
   continuous communion with God.

Unchastity is its own punishment
in that it makes the soul heavy and insensible
    to spiritual joys.

Unchastity infects the will with weakness,
pollutes the memory,
and darkens the imagination.
Even the body is affected adversely by unchastity;
it gives rise to psychosomatic complaints, fatigue
    and restlessness.
It weakens the body's resistance to illness
by strengthening the soul's collusion with sin.
Ultimately, unchastity foments unbelief, despair,
    and hatred of God.

To set out on the path of chastity
is to set out on the path of joy
that leads to the ineffable sweetness of union
    with God.
The soul is created for Truth.
The soul yearns for Truth
and recognizes Truth when she encounters it.

The soul that feeds upon Truth
grows strong in goodness
and radiates a supernatural beauty.
Unchastity blinds the soul to Truth.
The chaste soul holds fast to Our Lord's words,
"The truth shall set you free."

Unchastity produces, in the worst cases,
an aversion to the Truth
and a contempt for Truth that causes the soul
   to repulse it.

Chastity flourishes in the light
and turns to it like the sunflower to the sun.
Unchastity darkens the mind
and causes the soul to prefer the cover
   of darkness to the light of Truth.
This is why unchastity always goes hand-in-hand
   with the vice of lying.
Unchastity finds it necessary to spin a web of lies
   around itself;
it thrives in the climate provided by error, lying,
   and deceit.

Chastity goes hand-in-hand with love for Truth.
It delights in what is beautiful
and pursues what is good.
It generates a climate of joy
in which the other fruits of the Holy Ghost
thrive and abound.
If you would be happy, be chaste.[13]

In Every Walk of Life

One of the most common misconceptions surrounding chastity is that it simply means avoiding sex before marriage. Little thought is given to the vital importance of chastity within marriage, both for the sake of a healthy marriage and for the meaning of the virtue itself. After all, chastity before marriage with all its rules and limits would soon become pretty meaningless if every sexual practice became permissible simply by putting a ring on a finger. Chastity before marriage is the training for chastity within marriage. Without the former, the latter will be impossible. Without the latter, the former is meaningless. Chastity is for all ages because it is inseparable from the universal call to holiness. As the Catechism states:

> All the baptized are called to chastity. The Christian has "put on Christ", the model for all chastity. All Christ's faithful are called to lead a chaste life in keeping with their particular states of life. At the

moment of his Baptism, the Christian is pledged to
lead his affective life in chastity.[14]

The reference to baptism by the Catechism is a
reminder that chastity is part of that training in the
"practice of the faith" that our parents and godparents
took responsibility for during the Rite of Baptism.
What we term "sex education" should, in a Catholic
perspective, really mean "chastity education" because
it should never be a "how to do it" guide to sex (that
would be an offence against modesty). Rather, it is
an education in understanding God's gift of sexuality
so we can answer God's call to love in a way that
is fully human, dignified, respectful and generous. It
is not the purpose of this short work to provide a
fully informed, age appropriate education in chastity.
I just want to offer a few pointers on how chastity is
important for different ages and vocations, drawing
upon the wisdom of the saints.

Youth

Chastity, like every other virtue, must be learned and
it can be properly learned only if instruction in the
truth is accompanied by the witness given by good
example and by opportunities to practise virtue in
steps of gradually increasing complexity. If someone
wishes to learn how to play a musical instrument,
it is not enough to teach them the theory of music

or the structure of the instrument. They also need a skilled musician to show them how to play and they need exercises to help them build up their musical skill, starting with scales and simple tunes and steadily moving on to pieces of greater complexity. To teach a young person chastity requires the same approach. And who else can combine instruction and example as well as parents by showing love in the home and by sharing with their children at the appropriate time the wisdom of Christian teaching and practice? It is important that children receive education on the meaning of love, marriage, sexuality and procreation in a way that is suitable for their age. This means avoiding two extremes: prudishness and immodesty. Excessive prudishness and a total refusal to speak about sexuality, denouncing even mild sexual content on television and switching it off without discussion, could create an unhealthy curiosity that could lead a child or young teen to search for answers from morally unreliable sources, for example, the internet or experimentation with friends. However, exposure to too explicit information too soon or a blasé attitude towards nudity or sexuality could communicate the attitude that sex is "no big deal". Things that are precious are normally treated carefully and we do not give just anyone access to them. By treating the body with the same discretion and reserve as we would an important treasure, we learn even subconsciously the sacredness of the body and of sexuality.

Sexuality as a Gift from God

Unfortunately, our modern culture has become so sexualised that it is impossible to keep youth totally isolated from immoral influences. The lyrics of pop songs, the plots of even daytime soap operas, never mind late night TV, and the deluge of sexually explicit material on the internet mean that the innocence of youth is like a lamb among wolves. Even if it were possible to totally cocoon a teenager from all these influences (and only the strictest home schooler could even hope to attempt that), some day they will have to face the world on their own. To resist it, they will need more than just the word "no". They will need a positive vision of sexuality as a gift from God to be used to express the deepest love possible on earth: the total lifelong commitment of husband and wife and their cooperation with God in the most sacred work of giving the gift of life.

This is vital by the time dating begins. There is not enough space here to develop St John Paul II's theology of the body, but that is the very truth that adults need to understand for themselves and then communicate to youth in simple language. Young people need to learn "the language of the body" and know that happiness can only be found if that language matches the language of the heart and mind. Their hormones will be pushing them to experience what the body is sexually capable of. But they need to realise that we are not just our bodies. We have a soul and a heart. These also have natural needs as does the body. If the body seeks pleasure, the heart wants love and the soul needs truth and peace. Happiness can only come when all three speak with a united voice; otherwise there is internal division and misery. As the YouCat teaches:

> People who look for sex without love are lying, because the closeness of their bodies does not correspond to the closeness of their hearts. Someone who does not take his own body language at its word does lasting damage to body and soul. Sex then becomes inhuman; it is degraded to a means of obtaining pleasure and degenerates into a commodity. Only committed, enduring love in marriage creates a space for sexuality that is experienced in a human way and brings lasting happiness.[15]

The Search for One's True Love

This is the vision young people need to have and really desire for themselves before engaging in relationships.

A young person who feels called to marriage should know not to date someone who they could never see themselves marrying. Don't date according to mere looks, disregarding the importance of true friendship, or think "this is just an experiment to see what it's like". Even first loves should be approached with high ideals in mind, although experience teaches that first loves are rarely the last. The experience of disappointment and heartbreak can be opportunities to realise how important it is to search for one's true love and how vital it is to keep chastity in that search because the greater the intimacy, the greater the hurt at separation. A teacher once communicated this by asking young people to glue two pieces of differently coloured paper together and then rip them apart. It was not a tidy outcome. Some pieces of each sheet were left stuck to the other. Neither page would ever be the same again. Any breakup can be heartbreaking, even when chastity is observed. But the more intimacy is shared, the more of the other you will forever carry with you and the more of your intimate self you will have surrendered, never to get back. It's very possible that the increasing rate of mental health issues among young people is not only due to the stress of competition (be it in exam results or striving for popularity on social media) or even substance misuse, but to the damage caused by the regrets and hurts inflicted by unchastity. They need to be told the full truth in a dignified and modest way. They need a beautiful vision of love and true self-worth to strive for, as well as the frank reality of the dangers they need to avoid.

Here again, modesty (the virtue of presenting something good in an elegant, humble and understated way) is the key companion to chastity, just as curiosity is the best ally of unchastity. Curiosity can launch a young person into exploration or experimentation, either alone or with others, that can lead to strong pleasures which are potentially habit forming. We need only recall Augustine being held prisoner by sinful habits as if by iron chains: "The enemy held my will in his power and from it he made a chain and shackled me. For my will was perverse and lust had grown from it, and when I gave in to lust habit was born, and when I did not resist the habit it became a necessity." Aquinas observed that the pleasures of the flesh are very strong because they are part of our human nature and the future of the species depends on their role in driving reproduction. "Hence it is that if the concupiscence of such pleasures be fostered by consenting to it, it will wax very strong, like a child left to his own will. Therefore the concupiscence of these pleasures stands in very great need of being chastised." The discipline of chastity is needed to keep natural sensual pleasures from forming the addictive and binding habits of sin.

It can take a lifetime to break evil habits that are well formed and it's easy to see how common such habits are becoming, especially regarding masturbation, casual sex and pornography. We have known for some time about the health dangers of promiscuity but now some US States are recognising pornography as a public health crisis due to the way it has warped the sexual attitudes and behaviour of young men in particular. Hence, the importance of avoiding curiosity by knowing what is good and striving to seek that instead. And if a young person should sin in this way, it is vital that they be taught the importance of making a good confession because this sacrament is indispensable for breaking bonds and restoring us to freedom.

The Friendship of the Saints

The friendship of the saints is important as we need not just role models but intercessors. A boy should always be taught to love and respect St Joseph and take him as a foster father and role model. Let him seek the help of Joseph and he will not be left unaided. Similarly, girls should be taught to love Our Lady. One sometimes hears of Marian devotion being disparaged as if Our Lady is too remote or too unrealistic a role model because of her perpetual virginity. They forget that Mary is also a mother! Nothing of the body is unfamiliar to her or despised by her. Indeed, her chastity and motherhood together teach us the true meaning of sexual love as a service to life and ultimately to God the Creator.

The witness of the martyrs who strove to preserve chastity at the cost of their lives, including St Maria Goretti, St Charles Lwanga, St Agnes and St Lucy, cannot fail to inspire. More important, however, is the example of ordinary young people who led cheerful lives while being models of chastity. St Dominic Savio (1842-1857) was a normal teenage student with many friends. Yet he was always chaste, fleeing from filthy talk among friends and even refusing to go swimming if, in the circumstances, he thought impurity could happen. The power behind his goodness was his intense prayer life, especially the consecration he made of himself to Our Lady.

Blessed Pier Giorgio Frassati and St Gemma Galgani were ordinary in the sense that they felt the urges and temptations common to young people. Pier Giorgio (1901-1925) came from a privileged and powerful family. He wanted for nothing and could have led a life of carefree pleasure, yet he gave his life to working with the poor and Catholic youth. Like Dominic Savio, he was very prayerful and devout. He knew that the hot blood of youth can produce the fever of temptation that needs the medicine of prayer and the sacraments. He said:

> With all the strength of my soul I urge you young people to approach the Communion table as often as you can. Feed on this bread of angels whence you will draw all the energy you need to fight inner battles. Because true happiness, dear friends, does not consist in the pleasures of the world or in earthly things, but in peace of conscience, which we have only if we are pure in heart and mind.

St Gemma Galgani (1878-1903) was a mystic from the Italian city of Lucca. Even though she had intense spiritual experiences and would eventually receive the stigmata (the wounds of Our Lord) on her body, she was still very much a real woman with feelings and passions. It is no surprise that since she received so many graces from God and loved him intensely, the Devil tried hard to bring her down. On one occasion, she was so strongly tempted against purity that she fled outside and jumped into a barrel of ice cold water. She nearly drowned but the temptation was banished. Never underestimate the power of a cold shower!

The saints also offer advice on avoiding pathways towards sin. One of the visionaries at Fatima, little St Jacinta, stressed the importance of dressing modestly as a defence of chastity, stating that Our Lord is very displeased by immodest fashions. It is also important to avoid smutty talk or jokes. What we think, we become. If one's words regarding sex are cheap and degrading then one's actions are more likely to be open to sin too. As St Clement of Alexandria put it, "Filthy talk makes us feel comfortable with filthy action. But the one who knows how to control the tongue is prepared to resist the attacks of lust."

Those Discerning a Vocation to Marriage

While building upon everything written above, those who are dating or are in serious relationships need to live chastity even more intensely. The closer we become to someone, the greater the desire can be to express that love as fully as possible, to experience that sense of closeness and being loved in a physical way. The power of this desire cannot be underestimated. It is natural and only to be expected. But a prolonged struggle could be very difficult. That is why traditionally courtships were not expected to last too long. Modern life with its heavy economic and practical burdens means that early marriage is no longer an option. Adding to this the heavily sexualised environment created by the media, the influence of friends who are not practising Catholics, the easy availability of contraception, a generally permissive attitude (even from many parents), and the virtual expectation (especially for women) of having to be sexually available if you want to keep your partner, means that poor chastity is as endangered as the panda. Yet the situation is far from hopeless because with the help of God's grace all things are possible. As St Paul reassures us, "I have strength for anything through Him who gives me power" (*Ph* 4:13). It is vital to believe in the power of divine grace to help us in our weakness and to believe in our own dignity and goodness as children of God. Faith is not for cowards and surrender monkeys. But those who are bold in claiming their inheritance of divine grace and the assistance of the angels and saints have within them the power to overcome the world, even in the most challenging area of chastity: the power of faith (Cf. *1 Jn* 5:4). Didn't Jesus promise "Everything is possible to one who has faith" (*Mk* 9:23)?

To avoid a prolonged conflict, it is important that those in their twenties and thirties date the right person and not waste time on someone who is keen on intimacy but slow on commitment. Such relationships can lead one into sin and, at the end of the day, fail because of a lack of similar values. This requires looking for love in the right places. Membership of Catholic groups such as Youth 2000 or Pure in Heart and involvement in the life of the parish can help similar souls to meet the right person. Catholic dating websites have worked for many. Looking for love on dating apps that are normally used for "hooking up" is likely to be a dead end street for someone looking for a chaste relationship with a mature person who is ready for marriage. Indeed, leaving aside the danger of unchastity, such apps encourage a sense of vanity that feeds selfishness and thus undermine the capability for true love.

First of All, Seek Friendship

Perhaps the best way to find love is to first of all seek friendship. Indeed, if one wants chastity, friendship is vital because a lot of unchaste behaviour is simply due to loneliness in this ever more atomised world. As Dawn Eden has said of those caught in the vicious cycle of casual sex, "They feel lonely because they are not loved, so they lend their bodies to 'lovers' who do not love them". True friendship exists where there are common interests and values so that agreement can be built on the important things in life, where there is mutual respect and moral strengthening, and where love is characterised by a spirit of self-sacrifice. If any of these are missing, no matter how great the physical or emotional attraction may be, there is little hope of true marital love. The wonderful thing about friendship is that one does not have to go to bars or nightclubs to find it. The love of your life may be the girl or guy beside you in the lecture hall or at the next desk in the office or who you keep running into in the staff room or the gym. Why not engage them in conversation? Take things calmly and get to know each other gradually over a coffee, then eventually a lunch and later an evening out. Chastity reassures us that there is no rush, and in this sense it is liberating in the era of "speed dating". Even if attraction can be sudden, love must gradually unfold like a flower blooming in spring.

If long drawn out affairs are not advisable, neither is getting in too deep too soon. This is why sex before marriage and cohabitation are sinful *and* unwise. As we saw above in relation to Augustine, love and lust can create powerful chains of habit and necessity. Even when problems arise in the relationship that would make normal folk break it off, the unchaste can be blinded to the magnitude of the problems or delude themselves into thinking matters can be resolved simply because, deep down, they feel bound because of the bond that sexual intimacy creates. Intimacy can make one's partner act like a drug that one cannot give up. Marriage tribunals nowadays often encounter marriages that fail after a matter of months even though the couple may have been intimate or cohabiting for years. They have been caught in a drift:

they are hooked on one another, then when problems arise they try to resolve them by going deeper rather than by pulling back. Are things getting a bit dull or are tensions surfacing? Then "let's try new things" or "let's move in together"; then "let's have kids"; and finally "we might as well get married: doing things 'right' in the Church might fix it". It's like a gambler on a losing streak who can't cut his losses and walk away because he's already invested too much.

The Path to Marriage

We could do worse than heed the advice of Peter Ustinov when he described the path to marriage as being like a three speed gearbox: affection, friendship and love. "It's not advisable to crash your gears and go straight through to love straight away. You need to ease your way through. The basis of love is respect, and that needs to be learned from affection and friendship." This is simply the way of chastity: to respect each other and know that true love waits, taking time to explore friendship and common interests to see if you are suitable and having kept that bit of freedom so as to be able to walk away in time if you aren't. Waiting in itself is a good test to see if the other really loves you and will truly cherish you after marriage. We have often heard of young women being put under pressure to have sex with their boyfriends before marriage, fearing that if they don't the boy will dump them. If she says "no" and he refuses to accept it, then she will know that he really loved himself, not her. He "loved" her only insofar as she satisfied his desires. And he is foolish, because he could still have had the greatest thing: her heart, but rejected it simply because he could not have her body. Chastity frees you to genuinely love and it also provides the testing ground to know if you *are* truly loved. St Augustine noted: "It is customary for girls who are engaged to be married to delay the wedding for fear that a husband who has not suffered the trials of a long courtship may think his bride too cheaply won". If love means seeking the well-being of the other person then expressing love by means of sexual acts outside marriage is a contradiction. Such acts are mortal sins which, if performed with knowledge and freedom and not repented, will lead a person to hell. To ask someone to make love outside marriage is like saying, "I love you. Now can I lead you to Hell?" It's illogical as well as wrong. A firm, clear grasp of the unvarnished truth is as necessary as ever if chastity is to be kept.

Chastity in Continence

While they are awaiting marriage, it is important for couples to recognise how powerful temptation can be and so avoid occasions of sin, with particular caution being paid to nights out and weekends or holidays away. Chastity is so difficult today because an excess of freedom and a lack of accountability mean that couples have only their own virtue and values to rely on; hence the importance of self-awareness. One needs to have the virtue of prudence so as to recognise the situations where one could be tested and avoid them.[16] The maxim "Know thyself" is often the key to victory. St Philip Neri (1515-1595), the founder of the Oratorians, was a great pastor and spiritual director. His knowledge of human nature and spiritual wisdom meant he had excellent advice to offer his penitents concerning chastity. He used to say "In the matter of purity there is no greater danger than not fearing the danger: when a man does not distrust himself and is without fear, it is all over with him".

Engagement can be an especially testing time for chastity. After all, there is a ring on the finger. A commitment of sorts has been made and the couple may have the intention of being together forever. Against such temptations, the Catechism of the Catholic Church speaks with a very clear voice:

> Those who are engaged to marry are called to live chastity in continence. They should see in this time of testing a discovery of mutual respect, an apprenticeship in fidelity and the hope of receiving

one another from God. They should reserve for marriage the expressions of affection that belong to married love. They will help each other grow in chastity.[17]

Chastity as freedom is also important regarding cohabitation. If a couple decide to live together, and especially if they buy a house and take out a mortgage, they are already tying themselves to future commitments that aren't easily broken. This is even truer if they have children. By putting the cart before the horse by taking on joint obligations before marriage, they are limiting their freedom to break off a relationship if they feel that this is not really the person they want to spend the rest of their life with. The final furlong of the race to the altar tends to sharpen one's focus as the prospect of eternity together makes it all very vivid and real, banishing any immature romantic notions that held sway up to that point. We've all heard of engagements broken off at a late stage. Hence it's important to keep free of undue commitments so one can freely make a wise decision whether to marry or not. The consequences of bad decisions can be frightening because they are long lasting: "till death do us part"!

Married People

Marriage entitles a couple to be sexually intimate but it is not a carte blanche. The Catechism is clear that married couples are also called to chastity. Whereas all the unmarried are called to chastity in the form of continence, the married are called to "conjugal chastity".[18] This means carrying out sexual acts in a moral manner, in a way that respects the mutual dignity and well-being of the spouses and with due regard to the meaning and purpose of sex. A spouse who is attentive to the dignity of the other will respect their needs and frailties as they would want to be respected themselves. One cannot expect a spouse to be always sexually available to accommodate the whims of one's own lust. This would be demeaning and enslaving: it would reduce the other person to an object one can use as one wishes. Life will give rise to many occasions, be they of an emotional, physical or relational nature, where one spouse may not be able to have sex. A loving spouse will be chaste: he or she will be able to hold their desires in check and respect the weakness of the other, being content that the couple support each other with loving concern and chaste affection until the time when their sexual relationship can resume. Unfortunately, in some distressing situations (e.g. after a paralysing accident or a serious illness) the inability to make love can last a long time or even be permanent. Only the spouse who has already learned the art of chastity before marriage and practises it during marriage will be able to remain loving, chaste and faithful to their marriage vows in such a sad situation.

To live sexuality morally means being attentive to one's actions: that they are good in themselves and not objectively sinful. Thus even a married couple will refrain from the sinful actions enumerated in the Catechism, actions which of their very nature disregard the objective meaning of sex as an act that is designed by the Creator to both express love and create life. While couples may engage in some mutual stimulation as foreplay leading up to intercourse, such activity can never be engaged in for its own sake, independent of the marital act. For then pleasure would be sought for its own sake, with the procreative dimension of sexuality being deliberately excluded. This sin also happens when artificial contraception is practised within marriage. Blessed Paul VI in *Humanae Vitae* explained the reason why contraceptive sex is wrong:

> The reason is that the fundamental nature of the marriage act, while uniting husband and wife in the closest intimacy, also renders them capable of generating new life – and this as a result of laws written into the actual nature of man and of

woman. And if each of these essential qualities, the unitive and the procreative, is preserved, the use of marriage fully retains its sense of true mutual love and its ordination to the supreme responsibility of parenthood to which man is called.[19]

As Vatican II noted, this expression of mutual self-giving while remaining open to the will of God "is possible only if the virtue of married chastity is practised with sincerity of heart".[20]

The Habit of Chastity

The Church recognises that couples may need to plan and space births in order to be able to provide adequately for their family and exercise responsible parenthood. Provided it is not done out of a selfish motive, natural family planning (NFP) can be morally used within marriage. Natural methods depend upon chastity for their success. Only the habit of chastity can empower a couple to endure the sacrifice of abstinence at that time in the woman's natural cycle when she is fertile and conception would be possible. Chastity, since it requires mutual respect, good communication and honesty, is the bedrock of natural family planning as all these qualities are needed if NFP is to be used effectively. Chastity is honesty. St John Paul II expressed this well when he taught that the use of artificial contraception is a lie as it doesn't respect the truth that is expressed by the language of sex. He wrote:

> When couples, by means of recourse to contraception, separate these two meanings [love and procreation] that God the Creator has inscribed in the being of man and woman and in the dynamism of their sexual communion, they act as "arbiters" of the divine plan and they "manipulate" and degrade human sexuality – and with it themselves and their married partner – by altering its value of "total" self-giving. Thus the innate language that expresses the total reciprocal self-giving of husband and wife is overlaid, through contraception, by an objectively contradictory language, namely, that of not giving oneself totally to the other. This leads not only to a positive refusal to be open to life but also to a falsification of the inner truth of conjugal love, which is called upon to give itself in personal totality.[21]

Marital chastity helps us to see chastity not only as a virtue but as a fruit of the Holy Spirit. Aquinas taught that, as a virtue, chastity makes us live sexuality in accordance with reason, "But in so far as it delights in its act, it is reckoned among the fruits". Virtue of any kind tends to involve a struggle as we try to bring desires under control and live in a reasonable, moderate way. With the fruits of the Holy Spirit, there is no struggle by our reason and will, only a wholehearted choice that delights in something simply because it is good. The delight that comes from good sex, from being able to love one's spouse as freely and fully as nature intended, is a genuine spiritual good. It is a living in harmony not only with nature but also with God who is love. A love which is chaste, which is not enchained by selfishness but has been liberated so as to make possible the total gift of one's self to the other, is able to be in communion with God's love and so is truly happy. As Benedict XVI wrote, this love "is indeed 'ecstasy', not in the sense of a moment of intoxication, but rather as a journey, an ongoing exodus … towards its liberation through self-giving, and thus authentic self-discovery and indeed the discovery of God."[22] Here we can only glimpse something of the sacredness of sex and the childlike joy of those who, having conquered the tyranny of the flesh, live in the freedom of obedience to the ways of the Spirit.

Those with Same Sex Attractions

The teaching of the Church regarding homosexuality is challenging yet also compassionate. While the Catechism states that all sexual actions between people of the same sex are sinful because they do not respect the openness to life that is part of the natural design of human sexuality, it urges acceptance and compassion for those who have same sex feelings or inclinations, noting that these feelings are not freely chosen and can indeed be a trial for those who have them.[23] Like every other human being, "Homosexual persons are called to chastity. By the virtues of self-mastery that teach them inner freedom, at times by the support of disinterested friendship, by prayer and sacramental grace, they can and should gradually and resolutely approach Christian perfection."[24]

When the Church calls those attracted to their own sex to lifelong chastity, she is sometimes accused of cruelty and discrimination. Yet those who are called to the priesthood or religious life must also embrace lifelong celibacy. It is significant that those who are called to exercise the authority of teaching and leadership know in themselves the sense of loss and struggle that homosexual people feel. Some may object that priests and religious have chosen their vocation: they have freely renounced sex and family life for the sake of the Kingdom, while homosexuals have that renunciation thrust upon them. Those who make that objection have little knowledge or experience of the drama of a vocation. While some chosen souls may have felt called to priestly life and thus to celibacy from their early years and not have wanted anything else, I believe that most priests (and religious) experienced their calling, whether it came suddenly or gradually, as something they struggled to respond to. They were all too aware of their natural ambitions for prosperity and their desires for love and a family. They knew what they were being asked to surrender, but more than that, they knew who was asking that surrender from them. Can one say no to God? How will one answer for one's refusal on the Day of Judgement? Yes, one is free to walk away like the Rich Young Man in the gospel. But we know that he "went away sad". Deep down, the one who is called to leave all and follow Christ knows that he has two choices: surrender to God's will, or lasting unhappiness. That's not much of a choice! The only logical thing to do is take up the cross and follow Christ, even though the cost of sacrifice can be crucifying. By saying "yes" to his call, we discover a new intimacy with Christ, like the apostles who also left everything when Christ called them first and foremost "to be with him" – to be his friends, and only after to be sent out to preach (Cf. *Mk* 3:14).

Embracing the Cross

Those with a profound homosexual orientation are like those called to priesthood. They face a Hobson's choice: the acceptance of celibacy as a call to love in their own unique way, or to seek self-fulfilment in a way that defies the divine will. The latter is not a reliable path to happiness. The former brings that peace which the world cannot give but which Christ promised to his disciples. A few years ago, the editor of a British gay magazine, Matthew Todd, when writing in *The Guardian* had the courage to speak some unpleasant facts:

> There is this cliché that we are all having a great time partying, but actually we know, and the research is now showing, there are a hell of a lot of unhappy gay people; far higher rates of depression, anxiety and suicide than among straight men; far higher rates of self-destructive behaviour; substance abuse and sex addiction; and high levels of issues around intimacy and forming relationships.

While experiences of rejection and discrimination (which the Church strongly condemns) by family and by society at large may partially account for this unhappiness, it does not explain how unhappiness appears to be growing when homosexual conduct has never been as free or tolerated, to the point that it is those who oppose same sex marriage who are discriminated against, not those who promote it (as we have seen in many high profile legal cases, especially those of Lillian Ladele and the Ashers Baking Company). Could the answer be that the so-called "gay lifestyle" that is promoted by certain groups, with its emphasis on liberated or promiscuous sex, is profoundly unchaste and therefore damaging? The psychologist Alan Downs has touched on this connection in his book *The Velvet Rage*:

> Yes, we have more sexual partners in a lifetime than other groups of people. At the same time, we also have among the highest rates of depression and suicide, not to mention sexually transmitted diseases. As a group, we tend to be more emotionally expressive than other men, yet our relationships are far shorter on average than those of straight men. We have more expendable income, more expensive houses, more fashionable cars, clothes, furniture than just about any other cultural group. But are we truly happier?

The good news is that there is another way of finding love and self-esteem than isolating oneself in a "gay lifestyle" and conforming to its demands. There is the way of being accepted unconditionally for who you are as a unique child of God. The Church must tirelessly re-echo the words of Pope Benedict XVI's inaugural homily: "Each of us is the result of a thought of God. Each of us is willed. Each of us is loved. Each of us is necessary." In this sense of acceptance by the Church community, the person who feels alienated because of their sexual distinctiveness learns to accept him or herself. They also learn to accept God. If you can accept yourself as God has allowed you to be, then you can accept God who, for mysterious reasons known only to himself, has allowed you to share in the cross in this particular way. It is by embracing the cross in friendship with Christ who carried his cross and died for the sake of all of us, that one can also come to share in the power of his resurrection and so find joy. Chastity here means embracing the most elementary yet difficult truth of the Gospel: "Whoever cares for his own safety is lost; but if a man will let himself be lost for my sake, he will find his true self" (*Mt* 16:25).

"Friends of Jesus"

Much of the advice in the next chapter applies equally to every person of every sexual orientation who wants to live and love chastely. But for those struggling with various feelings and issues surrounding same sex attraction, it is vitally important to find a community that truly loves and supports you. That community exists in the Church in the form of Courage: an apostolate founded by the late Fr John F. Harvey.[25] The five goals of Courage were drafted by the members themselves and all five depend on each other for success. They are:

1. To live chaste lives in accordance with the Roman Catholic Church's teaching on homosexuality.

2. To dedicate our entire lives to Christ through service to others, spiritual reading, prayer, meditation, individual spiritual direction, frequent attendance at Mass, and the frequent reception of the sacraments of Reconciliation and Holy Eucharist.

3. To foster a spirit of fellowship in which we may share with one another our thoughts and experiences, and so ensure that no one will have to face the problems of homosexuality alone.

4. To be mindful of the truth that chaste friendships are not only possible but necessary in a chaste Christian life; and to encourage one another in forming and sustaining these friendships.

5. To live lives that may serve as good examples to others.

Anyone struggling in this area should read Courage's website and make contact so they can find the chaste friendship and spiritual support they need. While they seek acceptance for themselves, could I be so bold as to beg some acceptance and forgiveness for their fellow Christians who have not responded to their needs as Christ would have wished? The Church too has her wounds caused by the sins of *all* her members. Yet she remains the Body of Christ and an instrument of his healing grace. Don't forsake her! Don't let the prejudices of some Catholics keep you from the riches that Christ wants you to have through her liturgy, her sacraments and her communion of saints, both those living and those in heaven. Perhaps we could all learn from the example of St Teresa of Calcutta:

> During an interview, someone once asked Mother Teresa for her views on homosexuality. She announced that she did not like the word "homosexual." She paused the interview and told the reporters that if they had any more questions about "homosexuals," they would refer to them from now on as "friends of Jesus." This is how the Church invites us to view all people; especially those who might feel misunderstood, unloved, or unwanted.

Weapons and Remedies

In previous chapters we have already examined some ways of exercising chastity. Some ways, for example, prayer, are indispensable and are suitable for every person in every walk of life who wants to be chaste. Others might work for some but could be totally counterproductive for others. The main rule here is the rule of prudence, the mother of all virtues. St Augustine gives a very succinct definition of prudence as "love choosing wisely between the helpful and the harmful". It means applying our knowledge of moral principles to the individual situation at hand so that we can find the right means to achieve a good result. Just as unchastity destroys prudence and leads to foolish decisions, so too does prudence in knowing our weaknesses, what triggers our temptations and what is helpful for avoiding or calming them, help us grow in chastity. By praying for the help of the Holy Spirit, especially his Gift of Counsel, we grow in self-knowledge and in prudence. Thus chastity is a fruit of gifts and virtues infused in us by the Spirit. A few suggestions are offered here, but this chapter is by no means a definitive list of ways and means to grow in chastity. By trying them and by asking the Holy Spirit to guide you in the precise circumstances of your life, you will see what works for you and you may well find new strategies not listed here.

Embracing chastity might mean overturning not only an old lifestyle but even one's ways of thinking about sexuality. As we have seen, the world's ideas are very much opposed to Christ's on this subject. St Paul told the Romans, "Adapt yourselves no longer to the pattern of this present world, but let your minds be remade and your whole nature thus transformed" (*Rm* 12:2). This is the first remedy: think differently! To do this, we need to change what we put into our mind: new food for new thoughts. By reading this booklet, you are already availing of the first remedy: you are trying to fill your mind with what is noble, just, pure, true and beautiful (Cf. *Ph* 4:8). Keep up the reading! Read the New Testament and the lives of the saints, or the writings of the saints on the spiritual life. There are excellent books on living chastity by modern authors, for example Dawn Eden, Christopher West, Matt Fradd, and Jason and Crystalina Evert who also have an excellent website: *www.chastityproject. com*. Your reading will assure you that God loves you, that you are not alone, and that both divine and human help is available so that you can achieve the joy and freedom of a chaste life.

The Indispensable Power of Prayer

The most indispensable weapon against unchastity is prayer. Our Lord told us to pray at all times, especially not to be put to the test and to be delivered from evil, which we do every time we pray the Our Father. We must be faithful to prayer and not let boredom, distaste or even discouragement at our lack of progress tempt us into giving it up. St Bernard reassures us: "However great may be the temptation, if we know how to use the weapon of prayer well, we shall come off as conquerors at last, for prayer is more powerful than all the demons". This spirit of confidence and perseverance at prayer is essential when dealing with sexual temptations because they are so strong and addictive habits can be very hard to break. St Teresa of Avila encouraged people to keep praying if they had a long struggle because prayer and grave sin are mutually incompatible: one or the other will have to be given up by the end. As St Alphonsus Liguori said, "He who prays is most certainly saved. He who does not pray is most certainly damned."

Even though some types of prayer come easier to one person than to another, there are some prayers I consider essential. In first place, there is the Holy Mass, the greatest worship we can offer. Worthy reception of Holy Communion is essential medicine for the soul, particularly if we feel weak or strongly tempted to sin. Fr Ronald Knox called the Eucharist "the bread of the strong". He lamented that "Catholics are most apt to neglect Communion when they most need it; in the spring-time of youth, when the blood is hot, and the passions strong". It is important to lead young people to Christ in this sacrament and urge them to throw the whole burden of their lives on him, for if they receive him *with faith* he will be the satisfaction of their hearts' desires, their strength and shield. In the same proportion as we grow in devotion to Christ, worldly pleasures will lose their attraction.

Hence the importance not only of the Mass but of time spent in adoration of Christ present in the Blessed Sacrament. St John Bosco taught the boys in his care to make frequent visits to the Blessed Sacrament and to take refuge at Jesus's feet if they wanted to overcome the Devil and his temptations. Ven. Fulton Sheen did a Holy Hour every day of his priestly life and attributed all his success to it. Just as cancer patients rely on radiotherapy to shrink their tumours, so too does sitting before the rays of Divine Love emanating from the Real Presence gradually shrink our sinfulness and make us grow in our desire for intimacy with God, the source of all fulfilment. Sheen called it "cobalt therapy for sin". Next to this is the Holy Rosary. Our Lady is the Mother of purest love, and as Queen of Heaven she is all-powerful in her intercession with her Son. The chain of the Rosary is stronger than the chain of vice. St Pio simply called it "the Weapon". Because it's so humble a prayer, simply repeating Paters and Aves, casting ourselves with total abandonment into the hands of the humblest woman who ever lived, it is so powerful! St Paul said "When I am weak then I am strong". When we pray the simplest prayer in childlike trust and even weakness, God's grace strengthens us! Finally, I would recommend using the Holy Name of Jesus, especially in moments of sudden temptation. To simply repeat the name "Jesus" quietly and steadily with each breath can help to calm and focus us. The Eastern Church has always valued the use of the Jesus prayer: "Lord Jesus Christ, Son of God, be merciful to me a sinner" as a means of spiritual growth and even obtaining miracles.

The Beauty of Confession

After prayer, the most important weapon is frequent sacramental Confession. If we commit mortal sin, sanctifying grace is lost. The branch is severed from the vine, and in such a case Jesus warned "Without me you can do nothing". In ordinary life, if there is a power cut, the first priority is always to restore mains power. So too in the spiritual life: the mains must be reconnected by sincere repentance and sacramental absolution. Then not only are our sins forgiven, we also receive new strength to fight again and better resist future temptations. People tend to be embarrassed about confessing sexual sins and this is particularly true of youth. They feel shame very deeply and worry what the priest will think of them. That is why they need to be reassured that the priest isn't their judge but the representative of Christ and so is only concerned to minister Christ's healing mercy. And the priest was once young himself: maybe he remembers all too well some nervous confessions from his past. There is nothing you can tell him in this sacrament that he has not heard many times before. Do not be afraid. Just be honest: more healing comes from an open confession than a cautious, half-concealed one. Just name the sins as they are, without gloss. You don't have to go into lots of detail: just name the sins precisely and say how often you committed them. That is enough. If one is struggling with a sin repeatedly, for example, pornography or masturbation, it is good to have a regular confessor who is wise, can help you grow step by step, and will be there to encourage you if you have setbacks. Counsellors advise having an "accountability buddy" for these addictions and a regular confessor can fulfil this role as well as grant absolution. St Philip Neri knew this: "In trying to get rid of bad habits, it is of the greatest importance not to put off going to confession after a fall, and also to keep to the same confessor". Confession also helps us to know ourselves better and to become ever more humble as we tell our humiliating secrets. In our humility and our experience of being "mercied" in confession, we can also become more merciful to others who struggle. St Philip stressed this: "One of the most efficacious means of keeping ourselves chaste is to have compassion for those who fall through their frailty, and never to boast in the least of being free, but with all humility to acknowledge that whatever we have is from the mercy of God".

Weapons for Chastity: Halt

Two words sum up the best psychological weapons for chastity: Halt and Flee. HALT stands for "Hungry, Angry, Lonely and Tired". When we feel bad we act like little children and turn to the "pleasure principle": the things that will make us feel good. For some, this could be alcohol or drugs, for others it could be porn or sexual activity. I know that many Church Fathers recommended fasting as a remedy for impurity. Our Lord himself said there are demons that can only be driven out by fasting and prayer (*Mt* 17:21). Fasting as part of a disciplined life is good but sometimes it's not enough. St Jerome (347-420) fasted and prayed to be delivered from temptation in his cave in Bethlehem and what did he find? His mind was even more filled with visions of Roman dancing girls: "My face was pale and my frame chilled with fasting; yet my mind was burning with desire". Sometimes, as the great monk of the early Church, St John Cassian noted, we need to eat healthily (but never as gluttons!) because when the body is refreshed, the spirit is stronger for tackling the problem.

Anger (especially stress) makes us vulnerable to unchastity. That's the time to do something that calms you down, whether it is physical exercise or play a musical instrument or meet with a friend, etc. Here, prudence is most important as some types of music might seem enjoyable even though they increase our passions, or exercise might only get the blood up even more rather than provide a calming release.

Friendship is the best remedy for loneliness. It is as essential to a good life as food and water. But here too, prudence is key. A friend to whom one feels sexually attracted or who has similar struggles might only lead you into sin rather than out of it. Choose your friends wisely and always remember that no matter how sweetly you might feel about another, if the relationship does not involve true virtue and mutual charity and if it weakens rather than strengthens you, it is not a true friendship and should be broken.

Tiredness is another vulnerability, so aim for a regular bedtime and keep all entertainment media out of the bedroom. It is important to make sure tiredness never becomes sloth: contentment with lazing around, finding no enjoyment in ordinary, innocent pleasures, but always restless for excitement or something new. The Devil makes work for idle hands. Therefore practical hobbies, study and spiritual reading are most important. St Jerome learned Hebrew to keep his mind occupied and away from his lustful fantasies and this made him a great biblical scholar. Who knows what one could achieve through the good works taken on as diversions from temptation?

Weapons for Chastity: Flee

"Flee" is the most common advice given by the saints for dealing with sexual temptations. The Desert Father, Arsenius, heard God advising him "Flee, be silent, pray always, for these are the sources of sinlessness". In the spiritual classic *Spiritual Combat,* we are told to never confront impure temptations directly but flee from every occasion and person that could lead to sin. St Philip agreed: "When a person puts himself in an occasion of sin, saying 'I shall not fall, I shall not commit it', it is an almost infallible sign that he will fall, and with all the greater damage to his soul". Instead, he insisted: "In the warfare of the flesh, only cowards gain the victory; that is to say those who flee". This could mean changing TV or radio channels or switching off the computer to avoid impure music or images, or avoiding the company of someone who is a danger to chastity, especially if you are married. The evangelist Billy Graham avoided the scandalous affairs that ruined so many of his colleagues by never having a meal or travelling in a car alone with any woman other than his wife. In fleeing, he was safe.

However, we must flee *to* something good and not just away from the evil. We must flee to God. Temptations against chastity can never be forced out of our mind by direct combat. St Clement Hofbauer said when we find bad thoughts in our mind, we should think of them "as little as we do of the leaves that fall from trees. We must not dwell on them for a moment and … go quietly on our way." We crowd out impure thoughts by filling the mind with good ones. That is why St Benedict taught in his Rule that we should grasp evil thoughts as soon as they arise and "dash them to pieces on the rock that is Christ". I believe Christ is the rock described in Daniel 2:35 – the stone that grew to become a mountain filling the whole earth. We must bring our minds to Christ when temptations come and let our meditation on his presence grow to fill the mind so that it crowds out all else. This requires the help of spiritual reading and the discipline of mental prayer, which can be built up over time.

There are many stories of saints who exercised serious self-discipline to become chaste: St Francis rolling in the snow and, like St Kevin and St Benedict, rolling in thorns; St Thomas More wearing his hair shirt; Ss Catherine and Clare using cilices and disciplines; Ss Jerome and Aloysius fasting and giving long hours to prayer, to name but a few. The Church would not advocate some of these methods today but it does still stress the importance of doing acts of penance as they help us grow in self-control and help us be more open to the graces God wishes to send us. We are supposed to do penance every Friday and during Lent at the very least. Other penances, tailored prudently to one's own situation, can be helpful but only if done with the permission of a confessor or spiritual director so as to avoid harmful excesses and the danger of pride.

"Do Not Lose Courage"

Finally, we need courage. St James said, "Stand up against the devil and he will flee from you" (*Jm* 4:7). We must have the courage to shout a clear "No" to temptation, trusting that we have the mighty power of Christ within us and that he will give us whatever strength we need to overcome the temptation. This is best shown by St Maria Goretti (1890-1902), an Italian girl martyred for her chastity at the age of twelve. When her attacker threatened to kill her if she did not give in to his lust, she resisted by insisting "No! It is a sin!" Her habits of saying no to selfishness and sin in everyday life and trusting in God at all times made her strong enough to resist the fiercest onslaught imaginable. Just say no. It is simple but not easy, as is always the way of the saints.

And what if you should fall? Get up and try again, no matter how many times you slip! God's love and mercy have no limits. Begin each day as a new life. Don't let your faith falter, but be faithful to the Mass and to regular Confession. In the words of St Francis de Sales, "Have patience with all things, but chiefly have patience with yourself. Do not lose courage in considering your imperfections but instantly set about remedying them – every day begin the task anew." May God, who has begun his good work in you, bring it to fulfilment!

Appendix 1: Examen

An examen is a prayerful reflection on one's life to help us see how close we are coming to our goal of a holy Christian life. This brief examen is meant to help you reflect on the matters discussed in this booklet so that you hear the voice of the Holy Spirit in your conscience, guiding and directing you in the ways of chastity.

Prayer and Attentiveness to the Holy Spirit

- Do I prepare my heart each day, through prayer, to be a dwelling place for the Holy Spirit?

- Do I call upon the Holy Spirit to direct and empower me? Do I pray to him before study or reflection and before making decisions? In particular, do I have a habit of praying when I feel tempted?

- Am I humble at listening so I can hear and heed the Spirit speaking through the Scriptures, the Liturgy, the guidance of my confessor and the advice of family, teachers and friends?

- Do I seek the advice of orthodox and sound priests? Am I faithful to my confessor or do I try to confess to many priests because I feel shame or pride?

- How often do I use the Sacrament of Penance? Have I ever made a dishonest or incomplete confession out of shame?

- Do I feed my soul by attending Mass each Sunday and Holyday? Am I careful at ensuring my soul is in a state of grace when I go to receive Holy Communion?

- How do I use the Sacrament of Confirmation and its graces in my life?

- Have I consciously asked the Holy Spirit for his gifts and his fruits?

- Am I honest at examining the fruits of my day/life? Can I admit that my failures and feelings of sadness, emptiness and melancholy could be the Spirit prompting me to give up unhealthy relationships, habits or pastimes?

- Am I joyful, for joy is the infallible sign of the presence of the Holy Spirit?

The Passions and Appetites

- Do I try and regulate, in moderation, my intake of food and drink?

- Am I modest, especially regarding my dress and demeanour?

- Do I try to exercise healthily and lead a balanced lifestyle?

- Do I try to get enough sleep?

- Do I avoid laziness and sloth?

- Do I avoid any stimuli which may lead me into temptation, especially music, television, books and material online?

- How do I deal with anger and stressful situations? Do I bring them to prayer?

- Do I take proper care of my true friendships and avoid false friendships that harm my heart and soul? Am I prudent and moderate in my use of social networking?

- Do I seek to counterbalance loneliness by going out to do good for others and be part of the Church community?

- Have I harboured uncharitable thoughts and feelings for others? Have I been judgemental or lacking sympathy for others in their weakness?

- Do I try regularly to exercise some self-discipline, especially through Friday penance?

- Have I made time to fill my mind with all that is good and pure? Do I read the Bible, the Catechism, the lives of the Saints, orthodox spiritual works?

Chastity

- Have I stood back in moments of temptation and crisis and called upon the Holy Spirit or upon Our Lord's assistance and the intercession of the Blessed Virgin Mary?

- Do I tend to rely on my own strength, or do I seek divine help?

- Am I reckless and lack wisdom and prudence when facing possible occasions of temptation? Do I flee promptly to Jesus, Mary and the saints?

- How aware am I of my emotional needs and how I try to fulfil them?

- Am I afraid of loneliness and rejection so that I compromise my standards for love?

- Have I been prudent about how and where I spend time alone with those I am attracted to? Have I been careful about how much alcohol I drink in their company?

- Have I looked at others lustfully?

- Have I willingly engaged in sexual fantasy and day dreams?

- Have I used pornography?

- Have I engaged in masturbation?

- Have I engaged in oral sex?

- Have I had sexual intercourse with someone who is not married (fornication) or have I committed adultery?

- Have I had an abortion or advised someone else to do so?

- Have I used artificial contraception or encouraged someone else to use it?

- Have I engaged in coarse conversation or told dirty jokes?

- What is freedom, for me? Does it conform to what Christ teaches, seeks and offers?

Appendix 2: Prayers

In addition to common prayers such as the Rosary or the Chaplet of Divine Mercy, the following prayers are suggested for those seeking help with chastity. In addition to the many prayers to the Holy Spirit that can easily be found in a Catholic prayer book or online, the following devotion of Cardinal Mercier is excellent:

> I am going to reveal to you the secret of sanctity and happiness. Every day for five minutes control your imagination and close your eyes to the things of sense and your ears to all the noises of the world in order to enter into yourself. Then, in the sanctity of your baptized soul (which is the Temple of the Holy Spirit), speak to that Divine Spirit, saying to Him:
>
> "Oh, Holy Spirit, beloved of my soul, I adore you. Enlighten me, guide me, strengthen me, console me. Tell me what I should do; give me your orders. I promise to submit myself to all that you desire of me and to accept all that you permit to happen to me. Let me only know your will."
>
> If you do this, your life will flow along happily, serenely, and full of consolation, even in the midst of trials. Grace will be proportioned to the trial, giving you the strength to carry it, and you will arrive at the gate of Paradise, laden with merit. This submission to the Holy Spirit is the secret of sanctity.

While all Marian devotion is essential for a healthy spiritual life, the *Ave Maris Stella* is very powerful and Our Lady has let it be known how much she loves this prayer. Its reference to being freed from sin's blindness makes it a helpful prayer for deliverance from unchastity:

Star of sea and ocean,
Gateway to God's haven,
Mother of our Maker,
Hear our prayer, O Maiden.

Welcoming the Ave,
Gabriel's simple greeting,
You have borne a Saviour
Far beyond all dreaming.

Loose the bonds that hold us
Bound in sin's own blindness
That with eyes now opened
God's own light may guide us.

Show yourself our mother;
He will hear your pleading
Whom your womb has sheltered
And whose hand brings healing.

Gentlest of all virgins,
That our love be faithful
Keep us from all evil,
Gentle, strong and grateful.

Guard us through life's dangers,
Never turn and leave us
May our hope find harbour
In the calm of Jesus.

Sing to God our Father
Through the Son who saves us,
Joyful in the Spirit,
Everlasting praises. Amen.

Finally, the patron saint of chastity is St Maria Goretti. Here is a prayer for her intercession:

Oh Saint Maria Goretti who, strengthened by God's grace, did not hesitate even at the age of twelve to shed your blood and sacrifice life itself to defend your virginal purity, look graciously on the unhappy human race which has strayed far from the path of eternal salvation.

Teach us all, and especially youth, with what courage and promptitude we should flee for the love of Jesus anything that could offend Him or stain our souls with sin. Obtain for us from Our Lord victory in temptation, comfort in the sorrows of life, and the grace which we earnestly beg of thee (*here insert intention*), and may we one day enjoy with thee the imperishable glory of Heaven. Amen.

Endnotes

[1] YouCat 404.

[2] CCC 1832.

[3] CCC 690.

[4] See *1 Co* 12: 1-31.

[5] CCC 1831.

[6] YouCat 407.

[7] CCC 2351.

[8] CCC 2352. It is "the deliberate stimulation of the genital organs in order to derive sexual pleasure". Whether committed alone or with a partner outside of normal intercourse, it is gravely sinful because sexual pleasure is sought outside the sexual relationship in which the total meaning of mutual self-giving and procreation in the context of true love is achieved.

[9] CCC 2354. Whether real or simulated it is a grave offence as it takes sexuality out of the context of intimacy and mutual love that morality requires. It injures the dignity of those who make it and those who watch it. The YouCat calls it "a degenerate form of prostitution" (YouCat 412).

[10] CCC 2355. As in fornication, the other is reduced to an instrument of sexual pleasure but here even the semblance of affection – love is removed by commercialising the sexual act which should be a free gift of self.

[11] CCC 2356. As an act of violence it is a most serious offence, causing damage that can scar the victim for life. It is, I would argue, a satanic defilement of the gift of love which God intended sexuality to be.

[12] CCC 2357. Note well that the Church condemns homosexual *acts* because they are of their nature closed to life and cannot fulfil the integration of the threefold aspects of sexuality. She does not condemn sexual persons, emphasising that they must be treated

with "respect, compassion and sensitivity". They are simply called to chastity like every other person who is not able because of the nature of their relationship / status to express the integrated sexuality of a married man and woman

13   See Dom Mark's blog *www.vultuschristi.org* for many excellent entries on chastity.

14   CCC 2348.

15   YouCat 403.

16   See the start of the next chapter for a definition of prudence and further explanation of its importance.

17   CCC 2350.

18   CCC 2349.

19   *Humanae vitae*, 12.

20   *Gaudium et spes*, 51.

21   *Familiaris consortio*, 32.

22   *Deus Caritas Est*, 6.

23   CCC 2357; YouCat 415.

24   CCC 2359.

25   Please see their website *www.couragerc.org* which has help not only for those who have same sex attractions but also their relatives, friends and clergy who try to support them.